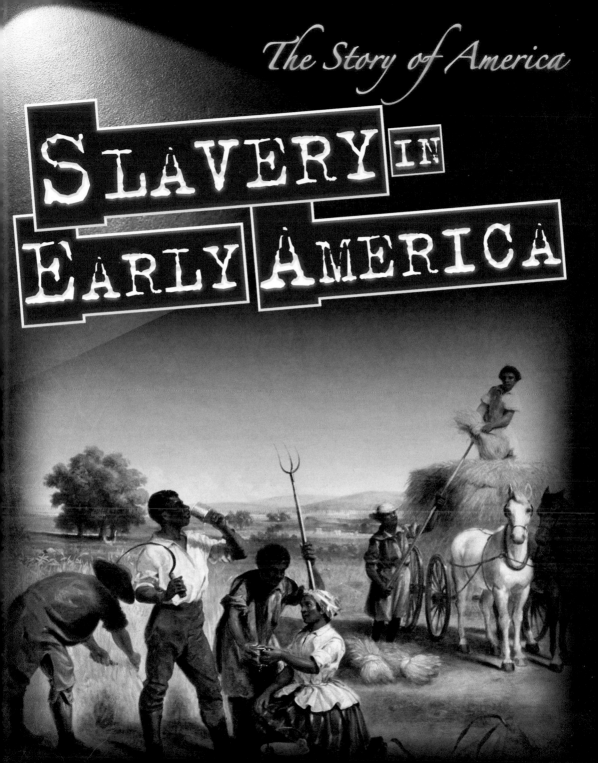

The Story of America

SLAVERY IN EARLY AMERICA

By Barbara M. Linde

Gareth Stevens
Publishing

Please visit our Web site, www.garethstevens.com. For a free color catalog of all our high-quality books, call toll free 1-800-542-2595 or fax 1-877-542-2596.

Library of Congress Cataloging-in-Publication Data

Linde, Barbara M.
 Slavery in early America / Barbara M. Linde.
     p. cm. – (The story of America)
 Includes bibliographical references and index.
 ISBN 978-1-4339-4777-3 (pbk.)
 ISBN 978-1-4339-4778-0 (6-pack)
 ISBN 978-1-4339-4776-6 (library binding)
1. Slavery—United States—History—17th century—Juvenile literature. 2. Slavery—United States—History—18th century—Juvenile literature. 3. African Americans—History—To 1863—Juvenile literature. 4. Plantation life—United States—History—17th century—Juvenile literature. 5. Plantation life—United States—History—18th century—Juvenile literature. 6. United States—History—Colonial period, ca. 1600–1775—Juvenile literature. 7. United States—History—Revolution, 1775–1783—African Americans—Juvenile literature. I. Title.
 E446.L67 2011
 306.3'620973–dc22

                                       2010039139

First Edition

Published in 2011 by
Gareth Stevens Publishing
111 East 14th Street, Suite 349
New York, NY 10003

Designer: Daniel Hosek
Editor: Therese Shea

Photo credits: Cover, p. 1 Superstock/Getty Images; p. 4 Rischgitz/Hulton Archive/Getty Images; pp. 5, 6, 9, 15, 25 (cotton gin) Kean Collection/Getty Images; p. 7 Buyenlarge/Getty Images; pp. 8, 21 (all images) MPI/Getty Images; pp. 11, 16, 18, 25 (signing), 29 Hulton Archive/Getty Images; p. 12 Life & Time Pictures/Getty Images; pp. 13, 27 Fotosearch/Getty Images; pp. 19, 20, 22, 26 Stock Montage/Getty Images; p. 23 Getty Images.

Printed in the United States of America

CPSIA compliance information: Batch #CW11GS: For further information contact Gareth Stevens, New York, New York at 1-800-542-2595.

Contents

Words in the glossary appear in **bold** type the first time they are used in the text.

Journey from Africa

The story of slavery in early America begins across the Atlantic Ocean. For years, the Dutch, Spanish, and Portuguese had been taking slaves from Africa to Europe. They also took slaves to their colonies in North and South America. The long route to the Americas was known as the Middle Passage because it was the middle part of a three-part journey. First,

Slaves were mostly kept belowdecks on the journey to the American colonies.

Europeans went to Africa. Next, they brought slaves to the Americas, and finally they returned to Europe.

Life on the small, crowded ships was unpleasant at best and often dangerous. The slaves were chained together with very little room between them. Their only food was usually a little bit of rice, beans, or yams. Seas were often rough and the voyage from Africa could take from weeks to months. Many slaves died on the journey.

Greek slaves

Thousands of Years of Slavery

Slavery has been practiced for thousands of years. African tribes often conquered and enslaved other tribes. It was part of war. This wasn't much different from ancient Greek and Roman practices. When they conquered new territory, they made some of the people into slaves. Slavery was used to punish some crimes and as a way to pay back money owed. By the time the Americas were being colonized, European royalty, church pastors, farmers, and businessmen owned slaves.

DID YOU KNOW?

Slaves were permitted on deck for short periods of time. Women and children were allowed more time than men. Sailors made the slaves sing and dance for exercise.

Arrival in the British Colonies

Because colonial record keeping wasn't exact, there are different ideas about where the first Africans landed in August 1619. Historians now think that a Dutch ship brought the first Africans to Old Point Comfort in Hampton, Virginia. About 20 Africans were traded for food. Governor Yeardley bought seven of them and took them by ship to Jamestown. Old Point Comfort is about

These men, probably Jamestown settlers, examine a newly arrived slave.

40 miles (64 km) downstream from Jamestown on the James River. No one is sure what happened to the other Africans.

Some of these first Africans became slaves. Luckier ones became **indentured servants**, with the hope of being free some day. This event marked the beginning of the slave trade in the British colonies.

Born into Slavery

In Hampton, Virginia, the first African child was born in the colonies sometime between 1619 and 1625. Records show that William lived with his parents, Antonio and Isabella, at the home of Captain William Tucker. At that time, Captain Tucker was in charge of the troops at Old Point Comfort. Later slave laws stated that children born to slave parents were slaves, too. No one knows the fate of young William.

Old Point Comfort

DID YOU KNOW?

The settlement at Hampton was started in 1610, just 3 years after Jamestown. At that time, it was called Elizabeth City.

PLAN OF FORTRESS MUNROE Vᴬ 1862.

Area of Outside walls 65 Acres. Granite walls 35 ft. high. Embrasures intended for 4. Ditch 75 to 150 ft wide. Tide ebbs and flows in Ditch 8 to 15 ft daily. 42 embrasures. War garrison 2450 men. Cost $2,400.000. N⁰ of Guns 1862 371. Many Embrasures were enlarged and heavier guns mounted (some 200 pdr Parrots) in 1862. was planned by Genl Simon Bernard Corps of Engineers formerly an Officer of French Army under Napoleon Foundations of the Fort were laid in March 1819 under Maj Charles Gratiot. The Fort was first ...ied by Battery C 3rd U.S. Artillery June 1823. Capt M. P. Lomax Commanding U.S.A. ...ie was occupied by a small Fort as early as 1608.

Slavery in Virginia

By 1619, Jamestown and the other Virginia settlements were successfully growing tobacco and other crops. At first, men from England **immigrated** to work in the fields. England was overpopulated, and colonial companies offered land to newcomers. However, the number of workers couldn't meet the demand for field laborers.

This painting shows Jamestown, the first permanent English settlement, around 1615. It was an ideal location for growing and exporting crops.

Growing tobacco and other crops was difficult. When the planters didn't have enough colonial workers or indentured servants, they began buying more African slaves. They paid with tobacco and other crops.

By 1649, records show that the number of slaves in Virginia had jumped to about 300. The number kept growing. By 1671, Virginia had about 2,000 slaves. The slave traders were able to supply as many slaves as the colonists wanted, and the colonists continued to want more.

Tobacco

John Rolfe—best known as the husband of Pocahontas—began growing tobacco in Jamestown in 1612. The tobacco plants grew well, and he soon took some of the tobacco to Europe. Tobacco became popular in England. King James I didn't like tobacco, but it made him rich. In 1619, Jamestown sent 10 tons to Europe. In 1639, farmers exported 750 tons of tobacco!

John Rolfe ▼

Pocahontas ▼

DID YOU KNOW?

Growing tobacco became so profitable that farmers had to be ordered by law to grow food crops.

The Spread of Slavery

As more colonists arrived in North America, more settlements sprang up along the eastern coast. Fertile soil ensured that more large farms and plantations were established. Slave traders brought thousands more Africans to the new colonies.

Samuel Maverick became the first slaveholder of the New England colonies when he arrived with two slaves in 1624. At the same time, Dutch settlers in New York began using slaves on their farms. Maryland and Massachusetts welcomed the slave trade in 1634. They were joined in 1645 by New Hampshire.

Numbers

Around the time of the American Revolution, most slaves lived in Virginia and Maryland. In fact, the slave population made up more than half of the total population of the Chesapeake Bay area. Only a few plantations had large numbers of slaves. Most colonists didn't own slaves at all.

The use of slaves became a common practice in all of the colonies. By 1700, there were 28,000 slaves in the British colonies. About 23,000 of these lived in the South. The number of slaves kept rising.

The number of slaves on a plantation depended on its size, the amount of work to be done, and the wealth of the owner.

DID YOU KNOW?

Slaves who were considered likely to flee were forced to wear bells. The ringing bells made runaways easier to find.

Slave Auctions

Slaves were often sold at **auctions**. After a slave ship docked, the Africans were led off and gathered into a pen. They were washed and their skin oiled so they would look healthy. They were often branded with a hot iron, so people would know they were slaves even if they escaped.

A family of slaves stands in front of bidders at a slave auction in early America.

Then the slaves were forced to stand on a raised platform, where buyers could view them. A buyer might make a slave turn around or check inside the slave's mouth. The buyers wanted to purchase the healthiest, strongest slaves possible.

Each slave was sold to the highest bidder. Families were torn apart. Parents and children were often separated forever. It was a frightening experience, especially as most slaves couldn't understand the languages spoken.

Escapes

Some slave owners tried to buy whole families. Most didn't do this out of kindness. Having a whole family of slaves reduced the chance that a slave would try to escape. Female slaves usually didn't run away if they had children or a husband. Young, single men were most likely to flee. However, it was too expensive for most colonists to buy whole families.

DID YOU KNOW?

Healthy young men usually brought the highest prices at a slave auction—about $100 per man in the mid-1600s. Women and children were less expensive.

100 DOLLS. REWARD.

RAN AWAY

From me, on Saturday, the 19th inst.,

Negro Boy Robert Porter, aged 19; heavy, stoutly made; dark chestnut complexion; rather sullen countenance, with a down look; face large; head low on the shoulders. I believe he entered the City of Washington on Sunday evening, 20th inst. He has changed his dress probably, except his boots, which were new and heavy.

I will give $50 if taken and secured in the District of Columbia, or $100 if taken north of the District, and secured in each case and delivered before the reward shall be good.

Dr. J. W. THOMAS.

Pomunky P. O., Charles Co., Md.

Slave Laws

There weren't laws about slaves in the early colonies. For many years, the differences between indentured servants and slaves weren't clear. Things began to change in 1641. That's when Massachusetts passed the first law that said selling, buying, and owning slaves was legal. That same year, a Virginia law made it illegal to help runaway slaves.

Virginia established the Slave Codes of 1705. They said all slaves would be treated as property. Any servants who weren't Christians in their native countries would be considered slaves. The codes gave owners the right to punish their slaves in whatever ways they wanted. They could even kill their slaves and the law would support them. Before long, other colonies made similar laws.

DID YOU KNOW?

Before the Slave Codes, slaves in Virginia could take their owners to court. A judge would decide who was right or wrong. After 1705, slaves couldn't go to court.

The dream of freedom made many slaves run away, despite the risk of beatings or worse punishments if they were caught.

Unequal Justice

John Punch was an African indentured servant in Jamestown. He ran away with two white indentured servants. They were captured in Maryland and brought before a court in Virginia in 1640. They were all sentenced to be whipped 30 times. In addition, the white servants had to work 4 additional years, while the judge sentenced John to be a slave for the rest of his life.

Life as a Field Worker

Most of the slaves in the southern colonies worked as field slaves on tobacco plantations or on farms. They worked all year long, from dawn until after the sun went down, 6 or 7 days a week. They tilled the soil, planted seeds, weeded the fields, and harvested crops. The owner

This picture from around 1800 shows slaves working on a cotton plantation.

or **overseer** told them what to do—they couldn't pick the job they wanted. Usually they were only allowed to rest for a few minutes. No matter how they felt, the slaves had to work.

The amount of food, clothing, and shelter slaves received depended on their owner. Owners could sell slaves at any time, so families could be broken apart without warning. Some owners treated their slaves well, but others used harsh punishments such as whippings or starvation.

Maroons

Some slaves were able to escape into swamps or other unsettled areas of wilderness. They lived in small communities, raised crops and livestock, and stayed hidden. These people were called maroons or outlyers. Most maroons were peaceful, while others attacked plantations and helped free other slaves. Some maroons were eventually recaptured, but some managed to remain free. Maroon communities existed in Virginia, North Carolina, and Florida, and grew until slavery ended.

DID YOU KNOW?

Some slaves were purchased by antislavery protestors and set free. A few even raised money to buy their own freedom.

Domestics

Slaves who worked in homes or businesses—in both the countryside and the city—were called domestics. Most were women who were without families. They cooked, cleaned, made clothing, and took care of children. Male domestics took care of horses and worked in gardens. Others were hired out to work in shops.

Domestics often worked 7 days a week, whenever they were needed, even at night. They slept over stables or kitchens. Still, usually domestic slaves had more

Domestic slaves often cooked meals for their owners, but they might not have been allowed to eat what they made.

to eat, better shelter, and warmer clothes than the field slaves had. They were able to leave the house by themselves, most often to get food from the market. There, they'd learn about current events or about their friends and family members. They also had better opportunities than field slaves to help other slaves escape.

Phillis Wheatley

Born around 1754 in Africa, Phillis Wheatley was captured and brought to Boston in 1761. John and Susannah Wheatley bought her. Phillis quickly learned to speak and read English. The Wheatleys were fond of her and allowed her to study instead of work. In 1773, Phillis's book, *Poems on Various Subjects*, was published. She was the first black, first slave, and third woman in the United States to be published. John Wheatley freed her that same year.

DID YOU KNOW?

It was against the law in most colonies to teach slaves to read or write.

Phillis Wheatley ▶

The Early Abolitionists

After the practice of slavery began in the American colonies, people calling themselves abolitionists began to speak against it. Members of Pennsylvania's Religious Society of Friends—or Quakers—became some of the loudest voices in the fight against slavery. Early Quaker settlers had been slave owners and slave traders. However, in 1688, several Quakers wrote the first North American document stating that slavery was wrong. Quaker Anthony Benezet founded a group that became the Pennsylvania Abolition Society in 1773. It was the first such group in the colonies and helped organize abolition movements in other areas.

The abolitionist movement continued to grow. Some first tried to pass laws stopping the importing of slaves. In 1769, Thomas Jefferson unsuccessfully offered such a bill to the Virginia government. It was the outbreak of the American Revolution that would begin change in the colonies.

Thomas Jefferson ▶

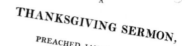

Printed materials helped spread ideas about abolition and the evils of slavery.

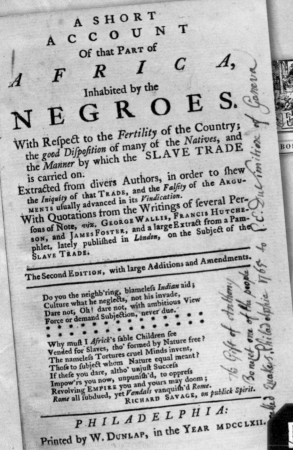

A SHORT ACCOUNT Of that PART of AFRICA, Inhabited by the NEGROES.

With Respect to the *Fertility* of the Country; the *good Disposition* of many of the *Natives*, and the *Manner* by which the SLAVE TRADE is carried on.

Extracted from divers Authors, in order to shew the *Iniquity* of that TRADE, and the *Falsity* of the ARGUMENTS usually advanced in its *Vindication*.

With Quotations from the Writings of several Persons of Note, *viz.* GEORGE WALLIS, FRANCIS HUTCHESON, and JAMES FOSTER, and a large Extract from a Pamphlet, lately published in *London*, on the Subject of the SLAVE TRADE.

The Second EDITION, with large Additions and Amendments.

Do you the neighb'ring, blameless *Indian* aid;
Culture what he neglects, not his invade,
Dare not, Oh! dare not, with ambitious View
Force or demand Subjection, never due.'

Why must I *Africk's* fable Children see
Vended for Slaves, tho' formed by Nature free?
The nameless Tortures cruel Minds invent,
Those to subject whom Nature equal meant?
If these you dare, altho' unjust Success
Impow'rs you now, unpunish'd, to oppress
Revolving EMPIRE you and yours may doom;
Rome all subdued, yet *Vandals* vanquish'd *Rome*.
RICHARD SAVAGE, *on publick Spirit.*

PHILADELPHIA:
Printed by W. DUNLAP, in the YEAR MDCCLXII.

E LIBERATOR.

Our Country is the World, our Countrymen are all Mankind.

BOSTON, FRIDAY, JANUARY 21, 1859.

A

THANKSGIVING SERMON,

PREACHED JANUARY 1, 1808,

In St. Thomas's, or the African Episcopal, Church, Philadelphia:

ON ACCOUNT OF

THE ABOLITION

OF THE

AFRICAN SLAVE TRADE,

ON THAT DAY,

BY THE CONGRESS OF THE UNITED STATES.

BY ABSALOM JONES

DID YOU KNOW?

In 1789, Benjamin Franklin became the president of the Pennsylvania Abolition Society.

Changing Minds

Those who depended on slave labor to run their plantations and businesses couldn't imagine life without it. However, more and more people were realizing that slavery was wrong. Even the Founding Fathers **debated** slavery. George Washington, a wealthy farmer, owned slaves by the time he was 11 years old. Later in life, his feelings about slavery changed. In his will, he set his slaves free, though not until after the death of his wife.

Slaves in the Revolution

During the American Revolution, slaves fought on both the British and American sides. Some fought in place of their owners. In 1775, Lord Dunmore, the governor of Virginia, declared that any slaves who fought with the British army would become free. Thousands of slaves escaped their masters, and

Many view the 1770 clash between British soldiers and colonists in Boston, Massachusetts (shown below), as the beginning of the American Revolution.

perhaps as many as 1,000 joined the British army. American general Washington later offered the same promise. About 5,000 blacks became soldiers in the **Continental army**. Some fought in **segregated** regiments, but most of the black soldiers fought alongside white colonists.

After the revolution, the number of free blacks rose from 25,000 in 1776 to almost 60,000 in 1790. The free and enslaved wondered if the new nation would honor the Declaration of Independence's statement that "all men are created equal."

Crispus Attucks

Crispus Attucks, a black man and runaway slave, was the first person killed in the American Revolution. In 1770, American colonists threatened a group of British soldiers in Boston, Massachusetts. The soldiers opened fire on the crowd, killing Attucks and several others. Some blamed the colonists for the violence, while others blamed the soldiers. No matter whose fault, the Boston Massacre—as it was later called—touched off the revolution. There's a statue honoring Crispus Attucks in Boston, Massachusetts.

DID YOU KNOW?

Former slave Salem Poor was praised after the Battle of Bunker Hill in 1775 for being a "brave and gallant soldier" of the Continental army.

◄ **Crispus Attucks**

The New Nation and Slavery

The American Revolution was still being fought when many individual colonies began to abolish slavery. The war ended in 1783. These colonies were the first to emancipate, or free, their slaves:

- Vermont (1777)
- Pennsylvania (1780)
- Massachusetts (1783)
- New Hampshire (1783)
- Connecticut (1784)
- Rhode Island (1784)

In 1786, all states except South Carolina and Georgia agreed to stop importing slaves.

When the U.S. Constitution was **ratified** in 1787, it still allowed slavery. In 1808, Congress banned the importing of slaves. Because the children of slaves who were already in the United States became slaves, the number of slaves continued to grow.

As the new nation added territory, questions arose about whether slavery would be allowed there. Compromises were made but continually caused conflict.

Compromising

Though a slave owner himself, Thomas Jefferson's first written form of the Declaration of Independence called the slave trade "a cruel war against human nature." However, some representatives from both northern and southern colonies refused to sign the document with these words. In order to get these colonies to sign and support the revolution, Jefferson took out the slavery section. Similar conflicts and compromises were made during the writing and signing of the U.S. Constitution as well.

the signing of the Declaration of Independence

DID YOU KNOW?

The invention of the **cotton gin** in 1793 changed the southern economy. With cotton as the new money-making crop, slavery gripped the southern states even more.

◀ cotton gin

The End of U.S. Slavery

With a growing number of slaves in the cotton-growing states of the South and West, the country could no longer stand united. The American Civil War erupted and was fought from 1861 to 1865. After the North's victory, Congress passed three **amendments** to the Constitution. Ratified on December 6, 1865, the Thirteenth Amendment abolished slavery in the United States.

Government agencies were formed to help freed slaves after the American Civil War. Here, an official stands in the middle of a conflict.

The Fourteenth Amendment became law on July 9, 1868. It granted United States and state citizenship to anyone who was born or **naturalized** in the United States, including slaves.

On February 3, 1870, Congress passed the Fifteenth Amendment giving African American men the right to vote. African American women—in fact, all women—got the right to vote with the passage of the Nineteenth Amendment in 1920.

Agreeing to the New Constitution

The eleven Southern states that had separated from the United States became known as the Confederate States of America. Nine of the eleven Confederate states ratified the Thirteenth Amendment in 1865: Virginia, Louisiana, Arkansas, Tennessee, Georgia, South Carolina, Alabama, North Carolina, and Florida. Texas agreed 5 years later. Mississippi finally ratified the amendment in 1995.

DID YOU KNOW?

During the Civil War, the Union held Fort Monroe on Old Point Comfort. Thousands of runaway slaves were protected there.

FREEDOM TO SLAVES!

Whereas, the President of the United States did, on the first day o present month, issue his *Proclamation* declaring "that *all persons he Slaves in certain designated States, and parts of States, are, and henc ward shall be free,*" and that the Executive Government of the United S including the Military and Naval authorities thereof, would recognize maintain the freedom of said persons. *And Whereas*, the county of *rick* is included in the territory designated by the Proclamation of the dent, in which the *Slaves should become free.* I therefore hereby noti citizens of the city of Winchester, and of said County, of said Proclam and of my intention to maintain and enforce the same.

I expect all citizens to yield a ready compliance with the Proclama the Chief Executive, and I admonish all persons disposed to res peaceful enforcement, that upon manifesting such disposition by they will be regarded as rebels in arms against the lawful authority of Federal Government and dealt with accordingly.

All persons liberated by said Proclamation are admonished to abstain from all violence, and immediately betake themselves to useful occupations.

The officers of this command are admonished and ordered to act in accord-ance with said proclamation and to yield their ready co-operation in its enforcement.

. H. Milroy,

Beyond Slavery

Right after the end of the American Civil War, there was a period called Reconstruction. The goal was to reunite the nation, rebuild the South, and help the 4 million **freedmen**. New Southern state governments built free public schools, allowed freedmen to own property, and made laws against cruelty to blacks. The freedmen were now allowed to travel, and thousands moved to Northern states.

However, segregation and **discrimination** continued for many years. In 1964, the U.S. Congress passed the Civil Rights Act, making it illegal to discriminate against people because of their race. The **descendants** of the slaves were finally and legally equal.

Timeline

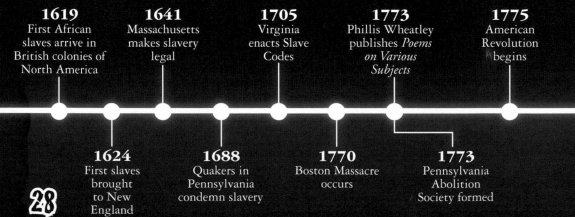

1619
First African slaves arrive in British colonies of North America

1641
Massachusetts makes slavery legal

1705
Virginia enacts Slave Codes

1773
Phillis Wheatley publishes *Poems on Various Subjects*

1775
American Revolution begins

1624
First slaves brought to New England

1688
Quakers in Pennsylvania condemn slavery

1770
Boston Massacre occurs

1773
Pennsylvania Abolition Society formed

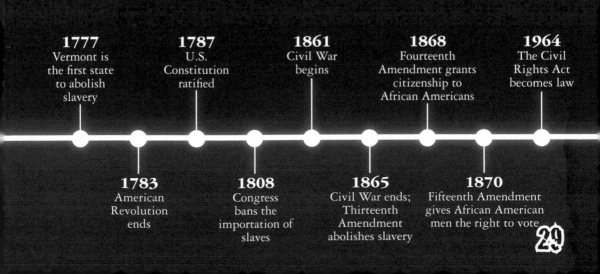

President Lyndon B. Johnson shakes the hand of civil rights leader Martin Luther King Jr. at the signing of the Civil Rights Act.

1777
Vermont is the first state to abolish slavery

1787
U.S. Constitution ratified

1861
Civil War begins

1868
Fourteenth Amendment grants citizenship to African Americans

1964
The Civil Rights Act becomes law

1783
American Revolution ends

1808
Congress bans the importation of slaves

1865
Civil War ends; Thirteenth Amendment abolishes slavery

1870
Fifteenth Amendment gives African American men the right to vote

Glossary

amendment: a change or addition to a constitution

auction: a sale of goods where buyers bid against each other

Continental army: the army of colonists during the American Revolution, led by General George Washington

cotton gin: a machine that separates the seeds and other small bits from cotton plants

debate: to have a prolonged argument or public discussion

descendant: someone related to a person who lived in the past

discrimination: unfair treatment of a group, usually because of race, ethnicity, age, religion, or gender

freedman: a slave who became free after the American Civil War

immigrate: to move into a new country

indentured servant: one who signs a contract agreeing to work for a set period of time in exchange for money or other benefits

massacre: the killing of a large number of people, especially when they cannot defend themselves

naturalize: to grant citizenship to somebody of foreign birth

overseer: a boss or supervisor

ratify: to give formal approval to something

segregate: to keep people or groups separate from one another, often because of race or ethnic origins

For More Information

BOOKS

De Medeiros, James. *Slavery*. New York, NY: Weigl Publishers, 2009.

Grant, R. G. *Slavery: Real People and Their Stories of Enslavement*. New York, NY: Dorling Kindersley, 2009.

Kamma, Anne. *If You Lived When There Was Slavery in America*. New York, NY: Scholastic, 2004.

WEB SITES

Africans in America
www.pbs.org/wgbh/aia
Learn about the history of slavery in colonial America and the early United States, including stories, timelines, and links to much more.

The U.S. Slavery Museum
www.usnationalslaverymuseum.org
Visit the Web site for the U.S. National Slavery Museum. See videos, exhibits, and much more.

Publisher's note to educators and parents: Our editors have carefully reviewed these Web sites to ensure that they are suitable for students. Many Web sites change frequently, however, and we cannot guarantee that a site's future contents will continue to meet our high standards of quality and educational value. Be advised that students should be closely supervised whenever they access the Internet.

Index